friendship

man

woman

friendship

marriage

family

These ancient symbols dealing with man have been collected from carvings, inscriptions and manuscripts. As a decoration for this book on friendship, one of these symbols was chosen. It is both beautiful and symbolic and part of a whole series of symbols telling the life story of mankind. The warmth and intimacy of the symbol complements the expression of friendship.

friendship

Compiled by
Ralph L. Woods

Designed by
Gary Carpenter

The C. R. Gibson Company
Publishers
Norwalk, Connecticut

To P. J.
Christmas 1970
From Larry

Behold, how good and how pleasant
it is for brethren to dwell together in unity!

Psalm 133:1

To a Friend

You entered my life in a casual way,
    And saw at a glance what I needed;
There were others who passed me or met me each day,
    But never a one of them heeded.
Perhaps you were thinking of other folks more,
    Or chance simply seemed to decree it;
I know there were many such chances before,
    But the others—well, they didn't see it.

You said just the thing that I wished you would say,
    And you made me believe you meant it;
I held up my head in the old gallant way,
    And resolved you should never repent it.
There are times when encouragement means such a lot,
    And a word is enough to convey it;
There are others who could have, as easy as not—
    But, just the same, they didn't say it.

There may have been someone who could have done more
    To help me along, though I doubt it;
What I needed was cheering, and always before
    They had let me plod onward without it.
You helped to refashion the dream of my heart,
    And made me turn eagerly to it;
There were others who might have (I question that part)—
    But, after all, they didn't do it!

GRACE STRICKLER DAWSON

A Prayer

It is my joy in life to find
At every turning of the road
The strong arm of a comrade kind.
To help me onward with my load.

And since I have no gold to give,
And love alone must make amends,
My only prayer is, while I live—
God make me worthy of my friends.

FRANK DEMPSTER SHERMAN

When friends ask, there is no tomorrow.

ANONYMOUS

I awoke this morning with devout thanksgiving for my friends, the old and the new. Shall I not call God, the Beautiful, who daily showeth himself to me in his gifts? . . . My friends have come to me unsought. The great God gave them to me. By oldest right, by the divine affinity of virtue with itself I find them, or rather, not I, but the Deity in me and in them. . . .

The laws of friendship are great, austere, and eternal, of one web with the laws of nature and of morals.

RALPH WALDO EMERSON

If I Had Known

If I had known what trouble you were bearing;
What griefs were in the silence of your face,
I would have been more gentle, and more caring,
And tried to give you gladness for a space.
I would have brought more warmth into the place,
   If I had known.

If I had known what thoughts despairing drew you;
(Why do we never try to understand?)
I would have lent a little friendship to you,
And slipped my hand within your hand,
And made your stay more pleasant in the land,
   If I had known.

MARY CAROLYN DAVIES

How intimately are we united when we truly meet in the love and presence of God. How well do we speak when our wills and our thoughts are full of Him who is all in all. Do you then desire true friends? Seek them only at the source of eternal friendships. Do you wish to hold intercourse with them? Listen in silence to Him who is the word, the life, and the soul of all those who speak the truth and who live in uprightness.

FRANÇOIS DE FÉNELON

There is no folly equal to that of throwing away friendship in a world where friendship is so rare.

E. R. Bulwer-Lytton

Friendship

Oh, the comfort—the inexpressible comfort
    of feeling safe with a person.
Having neither to weigh thoughts,
Nor measure words—but pouring them
All right out—just as they are—
Chaff and grain together—
Certain that a faithful hand will
Take and sift them—
Keep what is worth keeping—
And with the breath of kindness
Blow the rest away.

Dinah Maria Mulock Craik

Surely there is no more beautiful sight to see in all this world,—full as it is of beautiful adjustments and mutual ministrations,—than the growth of two friends' natures who, as they grow old together, are always fathoming, with newer needs, deeper depths of each other's life, and opening richer veins of one another's helpfulness. And this best culture of personal friendship is taken up and made, in its infinite completion, the gospel method of the progressive saving of the soul by Christ.

Phillips Brooks

Do not keep the alabaster boxes of your love and tenderness sealed up, until your friends are dead. Fill their lives with sweetness. Speak approving, cheering words while their ears can hear them and while their hearts can be thrilled and made happier by them. The kind things you mean to say when they are gone, say them before they go. The flowers you mean to send—use to brighten and sweeten their homes before they leave them. If my friends have alabaster boxes laid away, full of fragrant perfumes of sympathy and affection I would rather they would bring them out in my weary and troubled hours and open them, that I may be refreshed and cheered when I need them. Let us learn to anoint our friends beforehand. Post-mortem kindnesses do not cheer the burdened spirit. Flowers cast no fragrance backward over the weary way.

GEORGE WILLIAMS CHILDS

When your pocket's empty,
  when your heart is sad,
When fellow-men distrust you,
  your name and credit bad;
The man or woman who will then
  stand by you and defend,
Must surely be without a doubt
  a true and noble friend.

ANONYMOUS

The ring of coin is often the knell of friendship.

LA ROCHEFOUCAULD

Dan Paine

Old friend of mine, whose chiming name
*   Has been the burthen of a rhyme*
Within my heart since first I came
To know thee in thy mellow prime;
*   With warm emotion in my breast*
*   That can but coldly be expressed,*
*   And hopes and wishes wild and vain,*
*   I reach my hand to thee, Dan Paine. . . .*

A something gentle in thy mien,
*   A something tender in thy voice,*
Has made my trouble so serene,
*   I can but weep, from very choice.*
*   And even then my tears, I guess,*
*   Hold more of sweet than bitterness,*
*   And more of gleaming shine than rain,*
*   Because of thy bright smile, Dan Paine.*

The wrinkles that the years have spun
*   And tangled round thy tawny face,*
Are kinked with laughter, every one,
*   And fashioned in a mirthful grace,*
*   And though the twinkle of thine eyes*
*   Is keen as frost when Summer dies,*
*   It can not long as frost remain,*
*   While thy warm soul shines out, Dan Paine.*

JAMES WHITCOMB RILEY

A friend is a fellow who knows all about you, but likes you.

A TEN-YEAR-OLD BOY

The Friend Who Just Stands By

When trouble comes your soul to try,
You love the friend who just "stands by."
Perhaps there's nothing he can do—
The thing is strictly up to you;
For there are troubles all your own,
And paths the soul must tread alone;
Times when love cannot smooth the road
Nor friendship lift the heavy load,
But just to know you have a friend
Who will "stand by" until the end,
Whose sympathy through all endures,
Whose warm handclasp is always yours—
It helps, someways, to pull you through,
Although there's nothing he can do.
And so with fervent heart you cry,
"God bless the friend who just 'stands by'."

B. Y. WILLIAMS

A friend whom you have been enjoying during your whole life, you ought not to be displeased with in a moment. A stone is many years becoming a ruby; take care that you do not destroy it in an instant against another stone.

SAADI

Friendship has as many planes as human life and human association. The men with whom we play golf and tennis, billiards and whist, are friends on the lowest plane—that of common pleasures. Our professional and business associates are friends upon a little higher plane—that of the interests we share. The men who have the same social customs and intellectual tastes; the men with whom we read our favorite authors, and talk over our favorite topics, are friends upon a still higher plane—that of identity of aesthetic and intellectual pursuits. The highest plane, the best friends, are those with whom we consciously share the spiritual purpose of our lives. This highest friendship is as precious as it is rare. With such friends we drop at once into a matter-of-course intimacy and communion. Nothing is held back, nothing is concealed; our aims are expressed with the assurance of sympathy; even our shortcomings are confessed with the certainty that they will be forgiven. Such friendships last as long as the virtue which is its common bond.

WILLIAM DeWITT HYDE

The things which our friends do with and for us, form a portion of our lives; for they strengthen and advance our personality.

J. W. VON GOETHE

If, instead of a jewel, or even a flower, we could cast up the gift of a lovely thought into the heart of another, that would be giving as the angels must give.

ANONYMOUS

To My Friend

I have never been rich before,
    But you have poured
Into my heart's high door
    A golden hoard.

My wealth is the vision shared,
    The sympathy,
The feast of the soul prepared
    By you for me.

Together we wander through
    The wooded ways.
Old beauties are green and new
    Seen through your gaze.

I look for no greater prize
    Than your soft voice.
The steadiness of your eyes
    Is my heart's choice.

I have never been rich before,
    But divine
Your steps on my sunlit floor
    And wealth is mine!

ANNE CAMPBELL

Old Friends

We just shake hands at meeting
 With many that come nigh;
We nod the head in greeting
 To many that go by,—
But welcome through the gateway
 Our few old friends and true,
The heart leaps up, and straightway
 There's open house for you,
  Old Friends,
There's open house for you.

*   *   *   *   *

The many cannot know us,
 They only pace the strand,
Where at our worst we show us—
 The waters thick with sand!
But out beyond the leaping
 Dim surge 'tis clear and blue;
And there, Old Friends, we are keeping
 A sacred calm for you,
  Old Friends,
A waiting calm for you.

GERALD MASSEY

The comfort of having a friend may be taken away, but not that of having had one.

SENECA

Go often to the house of thy friend, for weeds choke the unused path.

RALPH WALDO EMERSON

Friendship renders prosperity more brilliant, while it lightens adversity by sharing it and makes its burden common.

CICERO

A Friend

There is no friend like an old friend
*   Who has shared our morning days,*
No greeting like his welcome,
*   No homage like his praise.*
Fame is the scentless flower,
*   With gaudy crown of gold;*
But friendship is the breathing rose,
*   With sweets in every fold.*

OLIVER WENDELL HOLMES

The most agreeable of all companions is a simple, frank person, without any high pretensions to an oppressive greatness—one who loves life, and understands the use of it; obliging alike at all hours; above all, of a golden temper, and steadfast as an anchor. For such an one we gladly exchange the greatest genius, the most brilliant wit, the profoundest thinker.

GOTTHOLD EPHRAIM LESSING

Greater love hath no man than this,
that a man lay down his life for his friends.
Ye are my friends,
if ye do whatsoever I command you.
Henceforth I call you not servants;
for the servant knoweth not what his lord doeth:
but I have called you friends.
. . . Ye have not chosen me,
but I have chosen you.

St. John 15:13-16.

The Friendship of Jesus

Thou mayest anon drive away the Lord Jesus
and lose His grace,
if thou apply thyself to outward things;
and if through negligence thou lose Him,
what friend shalt thou then have?
Without a friend thou mayest not long endure,
and if Jesus be not thy friend
before all others,
thou shalt be very heavy and desolate . . .
Jesus only is to be beloved for Himself,
for He only is proved good
and faithful before all other friends.
In Him and for Him
both enemies and friends are to be beloved.

Thomas à Kempis

Once in an age, God sends to some of us someone who loves in us, not a false imagining, an unreal character, but looking through all our human imperfections, loves in us the divine ideal of our nature. We call this rarest of persons, who loves us not alone with emotion, but with understanding—*a friend*.

ANONYMOUS

Four things are specially the property of friendship: love and affection, security and joy. And four things must be tried in friendship: faith, intention, discretion and patience. Indeed, as the sage says, all men would lead a happy life if only two tiny words were taken from them, mine and thine.

ST. AELRED OF RIEVAULX (CA. 1167)

Hearts are linked by God. The friend in whose fidelity you can count, whose success in life flushes your cheek with honest satisfaction, whose triumphant career you have traced and read with a heart-throbbing almost as if it were a thing alive, for whose honor you would answer as for your own; that friend, given to you by circumstances over which you have no control, was God's own gift.

F. W. ROBERTSON

Ointment and perfume rejoice the heart: so doth the sweetness of a man's friend by hearty counsel.

PROVERBS 27:9-6

What sweetness is left in life, if you take away friendship? Robbing life of friendship is like robbing the world of the sun.

CICERO

Cicero was the first who observed that friendship improves happiness and abates misery, by the doubling of our joy and dividing of our grief.

JOSEPH ADDISON

Old Friendship

Beautiful and rich is an old friendship,
Grateful to the touch as ancient ivory,
Smooth as aged wine, or sheen or tapestry
Where light has lingered, intimate and long.
Full of tears and warm is an old friendship
That asks no longer deeds of gallantry,
Or any deed at all—save that the friend shall be
Alive and breathing somewhere, like a song.

EUNICE TIETJENS

A friend is one who incessantly pays us the compliment of expecting from us all the virtues, and who can appreciate them in us.

HENRY DAVID THOREAU

We take care of our health, we lay up our money, we make our roof tight and our clothing sufficient, but who provides wisely that he shall not be wanting in the best property of all—friends?

RALPH WALDO EMERSON

What Is a Friend?

What is a Friend? I'll tell you.
It is a person with whom you dare to be yourself.
Your soul can go naked with him.
He seems to ask you to put on nothing, only to be
    what you really are.
When you are with him, you do not have to be on
    your guard.
You can say what you think, so long as it is
    genuinely you.
He understands those contradictions in your nature
    that cause others to misjudge you.
With him you breathe freely—you can allow your
    little vanities and envies and
absurdities and in opening them up to him they
    are dissolved on the white ocean of his loyalty.
He understands.—You can weep with him, laugh with
    him, pray with him—through and underneath it all
    he sees, knows and loves you.
A Friend—I repeat—*is one with whom you dare to
    be yourself.*

ANONYMOUS

One cannot be a friend without having one.

A. S. HARDY

Good Fellowship

Ho, brother, it's the handclasp
  and the good word and the smile
That does the most and helps the most
  to make the world worth while!
It's all of us together,
  or it's only you and I—
A ringing song of friendship,
  and the heart beats high;
A ringing song of friendship,
  and a word or two of cheer,
Then all the world is gladder
  and the bending sky is clear!

It's you and I together—
  and we're brothers one and all
When even through good fellowship
  we hear the subtle call,
Whenever in the ruck of things
  we feel the helping hand
Or see the deeper glow that none
  but we may understand—
Then all the world is good to us
  and all is worth the while;
Ho, brother, it's the handclasp
  and the good word and the smile!

WILBUR D. NESBIT

It is chance that makes brothers, but hearts that make friends.

ANONYMOUS

The best friend is an atmosphere
Warm with all inspirations dear,
Wherein we breathe the large, free breath
Of life that hath no taint of death.
Our friend is an unconscious part
Of every true beat of our heart;
A strength, a growth, whence we derive
God's health, that keeps the world alive.

The best friend is horizon too,
Lifting unseen things into view,
And widening every petty claim
Till lost in some sublimer aim;
Blending all barriers in the great
Infinities that round us wait.
Friendship is an eternity
Where soul with soul walks, heavenly free.

LUCY LARCOM

In the hour of distress and misery the eye of every mortal turns to friendship; in the hour of gladness and conviviality, what is our want? It is friendship. When the heart overflows with gratitude, or with any other sweet and sacred sentiment, what is the word to which it would give utterance? A friend.

WALTER SAVAGE LANDOR

A college friend of mine, devotedly fond of his friends, was also devoted to his diary. On a certain page of this he inscribed their names and arranged them in the order of his preference. Here he listed his (1) best friend; (2), next best; (3) third best, etc. though he reserved the right to shift this order now and then. He thought this an admirably clear arrangement, and was much surprised when he found that all to whom he confided his list were moved straightway to inextinguishable laughter! . . .

Your friends cannot be arranged in a row and numbered as first, second, and third because each of them is infinitely lovable, infinitely valuable in his own unique service to the rest of the world.

RICHARD C. CABOT

A Friend in Need

"A friend in need," my neighbor said to me—
    "A friend in deed is what I mean to be;
In time of trouble I will come to you
    And in the hour of need you'll find me true."

I thought a bit, and took him by the hand,
    "My friend," I said, "you do not understand
The inner meaning of that simple rhyme—
    A friend is what the heart needs all the time."

ANONYMOUS

Friends

Ain't it fine when things are going
Topsy and askew
To discover someone showing
Good old-fashioned faith in you?

Ain't it good when life seems dreary
And your hopes about to end,
Just to feel the handclasp cheery
Of a fine old loyal friend?

Gosh! one fellow to another
Means a lot from day to day,
Seems we're living for each other
In a friendly sort of way.

When a smile or cheerful greetin'
Means so much to fellows sore,
Seems we ought to keep repeatin'
Smiles and praises more an' more.

EDGAR A. GUEST

In the course of every friendship of some duration, there comes to us a mysterious moment when we seem to perceive the exact relationship of our friend to the unknown that surrounds him, when we discover the attitude destiny has assumed towards him. And it is from this moment that he truly belongs to us.

MAURICE MAETERLINCK

Friends come, friends go; the loves
*   men know are ever fleeting;*
In song and smile a little while
*   we read their kindly greeting;*
With warmth and cheer they linger near,
*   the friends we fondly treasure;*
Then on a day they drift away,
*   a loss no words can measure.*
This much we know: friends come, friends go,
*   as April's gladness passes,*
As sun and shade, in swift parade,
*   paint changes on meadow grasses.*
And though we grieve to see them leave,
*   in thought we still enfold them;*
In Memory's Net we keep them yet,
*   and thus can ever hold them.*
They come, they go—these Loves we know.
*   Life's Tides are ever moving;*
But year on year, they still seem near—
*   so great the power of loving.*

Author Unknown

It is one mark of a friend that he makes you wish to be at your best while you are with him.

Henry Van Dyke

Unless you make allowances for your friend's foibles, you betray your own.

Syrus

We can never replace a friend. When a man is fortunate enough to have several, he finds them all different. No one has a double in friendship.

J. C. F. VON SCHILLER

"He is my friend," I said—
"Be patient!" Overhead
The skies were drear and dim;
And lo! the thought of him
Smiled on my heart—and then
The sun shone out again!

JAMES WHITCOMB RILEY

A Common Friendship—Who talks of a Common Friendship? There is no such thing in the world. On earth no word is more sublime.

HENRY DRUMMOND

All we can do is to make the best of our friends, love and cherish what is good in them, and keep out of the way of what is bad.

THOMAS JEFFERSON

Friendship consists in forgetting what one gives, and remembering what one receives.

ALEXANDRE DUMAS

My Friend

It seems the world was always bright
    With some divine unclouded weather,
When we, with hearts and footsteps light,
    By lawn and river walked together.

There was no talk of me and you,
    Of theories with facts to bound them,
We were content to be and do,
    And take our fortunes as we found them. . . .

It seems I was not hard to please,
    Where'er you led I needs must follow;
For strength you were my Hercules,
    For wit and luster my Apollo.

The years flew onward: stroke by stroke,
    They clashed from the impartial steeple,
And we appear to other folk
    A pair of ordinary people.

One word, old friend: though fortune flies,
    If hope should fail—till death shall sever—
In one dim pair of faithful eyes
    You seem as bright, as brave as ever.

ARTHUR C. BENSON

Have Friends. Tis a second existence. Every friend is good and wise for his friend: among them all everything turns to good. Every one is as others wish him; that they may wish him well, he must win their hearts and so their tongues. There is no magic like a good turn, and the way to gain friendly feelings is to do friendly acts. The most and best of us depend on others; we have to live either among friends or among enemies. Seek some one every day to be a well-wisher if not a friend; by and by after trial some of these will become intimate.

BALTASAR GRACIAN

It is sweet to be appreciated by a great number and to be understood by a few.

ABEL BONNARD

The man that hails you Tom or Jack,
And proves, by thumping on your back,
His sense of your great merit,
Is such a friend that one had need
Be very much his friend indeed
To pardon or to bear it.

WILLIAM COWPER

We are all travellers in the wilderness of this world, and the best that we find in our travels is an honest friend.

ROBERT LOUIS STEVENSON

There is in friendship something of all relations, and something above them all. It is the golden thread that ties the hearts of all hearts of all the world.

JOHN EVELYN

There are no rules for friendship. It must be left to itself. We cannot force it any more than love.

WILLIAM HAZLITT

Friendship

Friendship needs no studied phrases,
*   Polished face, or winning wiles;*
Friendship deals no lavish praises,
*   Friendship dons no surface smiles.*
Friendship follows Nature's diction,
*   Shuns the blandishments of Art,*
Boldly severs truth from fiction,
*   Speaks the language of the heart.*
Friendship—pure, unselfish friendship,
*   All through life's alloted span,*
Nurtures, strengthens, widens, lengthens,
*   Man's relationship with man.*

ANONYMOUS

Instead of loving your enemies, treat your friends a little better.

E. W. HOWE

Friendship is a word the very sight of which in print makes the heart warm.

AUGUSTINE BIRRELL

There is no man that imparteth his joys to his friends, but he joyeth the more; and no man that imparteth his griefs to his friend, but he grieveth the less.

FRANCIS BACON

The holy passion of Friendship is so sweet and steady and loyal and enduring a nature that it will last through a whole lifetime, if not asked to lend money.

MARK TWAIN

My friend peers in on me with merry
Wise face, and though the sky stays dim,
The very light of day, the very
Sun's self comes in with him.

ALGERNON CHARLES SWINBURNE

If a man does not make new acquaintances as he advances through life, he will soon find himself alone. A man should keep his friendships in constant repair.

SAMUEL JOHNSON

I loved my friend for his gentleness, his candor, his truth, his good repute, his freedom even from my livelier manner, his calm and reasonable kindness. It was not any particular talent that attracted me to him, or anything striking whatsoever. I should say, in one word, it was his goodness. I doubt whether he ever had a conception of a tithe of the regard and respect I entertained for him; and I smile to think of the perplexity (though he never showed it) which he probably felt sometimes, at my enthusiastic expressions; for I thought him a kind of angel . . . With the other boys I played antics, and rioted in fantastic jests; but in his society, or whenever I thought of him, I fell into a kind of Sabbath state of bliss; and I am sure I could have died for him.

LEIGH HUNT

The making of friends,
who are real friends,
is the best token
we have of a man's
success in life.

EDWARD EVERETT HALE

Treat your friends for what you know them to be. Regard no surfaces. Consider not what they did, but what they intended.

HENRY DAVID THOREAU

Life is to be fortified by many friendships. To love and to be loved, is the greatest happiness of existence. If I lived under the burning sun of the equator, it would be a pleasure to me to think that there were many human beings on the other side of the world who regarded and respected me; I could and would not live if I were alone upon the earth, and cut off from the remembrance of my fellow-creatures. It is not that a man has occasion often to fall back upon the kindness of his friends; perhaps he may never experience the necessity of doing so; but we are governed by our imaginations, and they stand there as a solid and impregnable bulwark against all the evils of life.

SYDNEY SMITH

The tide of friendship does not rise high on the bank of perfection. Amiable weaknesses and shortcomings are the food of love. It is from the roughnesses and imperfect breaks in a man that you are able to lay hold of him. If a man be an entire and perfect chrysolite, you slide off him and fall back into ignorance. My friends are not perfect— no more am I—and so we suit each other admirably. Their weaknesses keep mine in countenance, and so save me from humiliation and shame. We give and take, bear and forbear; the stupidity they utter today salves the recollection of the stupidity I uttered yesterday; in their want of it I see my own, and so feel satisfied and kindly disposed. It is one of the charitable dispensations of Providence that perfection is not essential to friendship.

ALEXANDER SMITH

To a Comrade

The joy of meeting makes us love farewell;
We gather once again around the hearth,
    And thou will tell
All that thy keen experience has been
Of pleasure, danger, misadventure, mirth,
    And unforeseen.

*　*　*　*

But friend, go not again so far away;
In need of some small help I always stand,
    Come whatso may;
I know not whither leads this path of mine,
But I can tread it better when my hand
    Is clasped in thine.

ALFRED DE MUSSET

Once being asked how we should treat our friends, Aristotle said, "As we would wish them to treat us." Asked what a friend is, he answered, "One soul abiding in two bodies."

DIOGENES LAERTIUS

A man's growth is seen in the successive choirs of his friends.

RALPH WALDO EMERSON

The child alone is the true democrat; to him only is every-one he meets a friend.

ANONYMOUS

Who seeks a friend without a fault remains without one.

PROVERB

In prosperity our friends know us; in adversity we know our friends.

JOHN C. COLLINS

Two persons will not be friends long if they cannot forgive each other's little failings.

H. JEAN DE LA BRUYERE

There may be moments in friendship, as in love, when silence is beyond words. The faults of our friend may be clear to us, but it is well to seem to shut our eyes to them. Friendship is usually treated by the majority of mankind as a tough and everlasting thing which will survive all manner of bad treatment. But this is an exceedingly great and foolish error; it may die in an hour of a single unwise word; its conditions of existence are that it should be dealt with delicately and tenderly, being as it is a sensible plant and not a roadside thistle. We must not expect our friend to be above humanity.

OUIDA

A Town's Tribute to Its Friend

The other day in Emporia [Kansas], the longest funeral procession that has formed in ten years followed the Rev. John Jones three long miles in the hot July sun out to Dry Creek Cemetery. Now, a funeral procession may mean little or much. When a rich and powerful man dies, the people play politics and attend his funeral for various reasons. But here was the body of a meek, gentle little old man—a man "without purse or scrip." It won't take twenty minutes to settle his estate in probate court. He was a preacher of the gospel—but preachers have been buried before this in Emporia without much show of sorrow.

The reason so many people lined up behind the hearse that held the kind old man's mortality was simple: they loved him. He devoted his life to helping people. In a very simple way, without money or worldly power, he gave of the gentleness of his heart to all around him. . . . When others gave money—which was of their store—he gave prayers and hard work and an inspiring courage. He helped. In his sphere he was a power. And so when he lay down to sleep hundreds of friends trudged out to bid him good-by with moist eyes and with cramped throats to wish him sweet slumber.

WILLIAM ALLEN WHITE

No distance of place or lapse of time can lessen the friendship of those who are thoroughly persuaded of each other's worth.

ROBERT SOUTHEY

The most I can do for my friend is simply to be his friend. I have no wealth to bestow on him. If he knows that I am happy in loving him, he will want no other reward. Is not friendship divine in this?

HENRY DAVID THOREAU

The friends thou hast, and their adoption tried,
Grapple them to thy soul with hoops of steel;
But do not dull thy palm with entertainment
Of each new-hatch'd, unfledged comrade.

WILLIAM SHAKESPEARE

If we would build on a sure foundation in friendship, we must love our friends for *their* sake rather than for *our* own.

CHARLOTTE BRONTË

A really noble friendship, which realizes the higher ideals of the relation, must be open-eyed; friendship ought never to lose its sight. Our friendship is really helpful to others, not when it makes things easy for them, gratifying their desires and yielding to their humours, but when it develops the best that is in them; when it puts them on their mettle, makes their weaknesses clear, and spurs them to the acquirement of the strength which overcomes. "Our friends," said Emerson with characteristic insight, "are those who make us do what we can."

HAMILTON WRIGHT MABIE

Such is friendship that through it we love places and seasons; for as bright bodies emit rays to a distance, and flowers drop their sweet leaves on the ground around them, so friends impart favor even to the places where they dwell. With friends even poverty is pleasant. Words cannot express the joy which a friend imparts; they only can know who have experienced that joy. A friend is dearer than the light of heaven, for it would be better for us that the sun were extinguished than that we should be without friends.

ST. JOHN CHRYSOSTOM

My friends are little lamps to me,
*   Their radiance warms and cheers my ways.*
And all my pathway dark and lone
*   Is brightened by their rays.*
I try to keep them bright by faith,
*   And never let them dim with doubt,*
For every time I lose a friend
*   A little lamp goes out.*

ELIZABETH WHITTEMORE

A friend you have to buy won't be worth what you pay for him.

GEORGE D. PRENTICE

Convey thy love to thy friends, as an arrow to the mark, to stick there; not as a ball against the wall to rebound back to thee. That Friendship will not continue to the End that is begun for an End.

FRANCIS QUARLES

It is a good thing to be rich, and a good thing to be strong, but it is a better thing to be beloved of many friends.

EURIPIDES

The wise man seeks a friend in whom are those qualities which he himself may lack; for thus being united is their friendship the more completely defended against adversity.

JEREMY TAYLOR

"Now Is the Day"

You who are letting miserable misunderstandings run from year to year, meaning to clear them up someday; you who are keeping wretched quarrels alive because you cannot quite make up your minds that now is the day to sacrifice your pride and kill them; you who are passing men sullenly upon the street, not speaking to them out of some silly spite, and yet knowing that it would fill you with shame and remorse if you heard that one of them were dead tomorrow morning; you who are letting your neighbor starve, till you heard that he is dying of starvation; or letting your friend's heart ache for a word of appreciation or sympathy, which you mean to give him someday; if you could only know and see and feel, all of a sudden, that "the time is short," how it would break the spell! How you would go instantly and do the thing which you might never have another chance to do!

PHILLIPS BROOKS

ACKNOWLEDGEMENTS

The publisher and the compiler are grateful to the following for permission to use the protected material indicated:

THE BOBBS-MERRILL CO. INC., from *The Biographical Edition of the Complete Works of James Whitcomb Riley*, copyright 1913 by James Whitcomb Riley, reprinted by permission of the publishers, The Bobbs-Merrill Co. Inc.

THE BODLEY HEAD, London, England, from Arthur Christopher Benson's *Collected Poems.*

ANNE CAMPBELL (MRS. GEORGE W. STARK), for her poem "To My Friend."

GRACE STRICKLER DAWSON, for her poem "To a Friend."

HOUGHTON MIFFLIN CO., from Richard C. Cabot's *What Men Live By*, 1914.

MACMILLAN AND CO. LTD., from Joseph Jacobson's translation of Baltasar Gracian's WORLDLY WISDOM.

ALFRED A. KNOPF, INC., for "Old Friendship" from *Leaves in Windy Weather* by Eunice Tietjens, copyright, 1929 by Alfred A. Knopf, Inc., and renewed 1957 by Cloyd Head.

HENRY REGNERY CO., for "Friends" by Edgar A. Guest.

SIMON AND SCHUSTER, INC., from Abel Bonnard's *The Art of Friendship*, translated by P. P. Fallon, 1933.

Every effort has been made to trace the ownership and copyright status of selections in the book, to secure permission for protected material. If any errors or oversights have occurred, correction will be made in future printings.

R.L.W.